Pennsylvania Military Museum

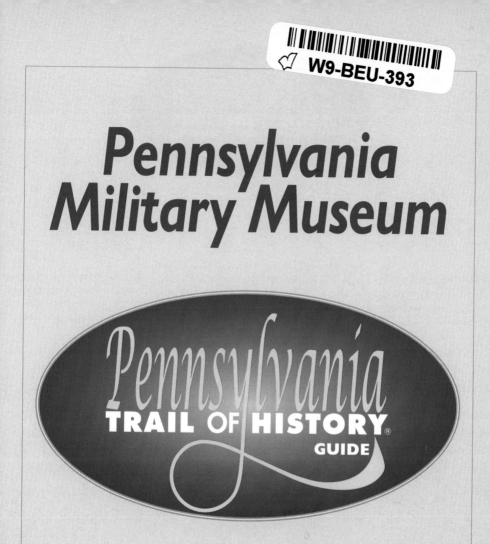

Pennsylvania
TRAIL OF HISTORY
GUIDE

Text by Arthur P. Miller Jr.
and Marjorie L. Miller

STACKPOLE BOOKS

PENNSYLVANIA HISTORICAL
AND MUSEUM COMMISSION

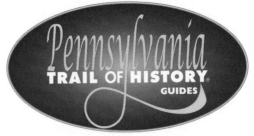

Kyle R. Weaver, Series Editor
Tracy Patterson, Designer

Published by
STACKPOLE BOOKS
5067 Ritter Road
Mechanicsburg, Pennsylvania 17055

Printed in the United States of America
2 4 6 8 10 9 7 5 3 1
FIRST EDITION

Maps by Caroline Stover

Cover: PENNSYLVANIA MILITARY MUSEUM
Page 3: 28th Infantry Division victory parade on Broad Street in Philadelphia, May 1919.
PENNSYLVANIA STATE ARCHIVES
Page 5: 28th Infantry Division victory parade in Paris, August 29, 1944.
PENNSYLVANIA MILITARY MUSEUM
All other credits are noted throughout

Library of Congress Cataloging-in-Publication Data

Miller, Arthur P., Jr.
    Pennsylvania Military Museum : Pennsylvania trail of history guide / text by Arthur P. Miller Jr. and Marjorie L. Miller.— 1st ed.
        p. cm.—(Pennsylvania trail of history guides)
    Includes bibliographical references.
    ISBN-13: 978-0-8117-3192-8 (pbk.)
    ISBN-10: 0-8117-3192-8 (pbk.)
    1. Pennsylvania Military Museum—Guidebooks. 2. Pennsylvania—History, Military. 3. Soldiers—Pennsylvania—History. I. Miller, Marjorie L. (Marjorie Lyman), 1929– II. Title. III. Series.

F146.5.M55 2005
355'.009748—dc22
                                                     2005009385

Contents

Editor's Preface

Pennsylvania has a strong military tradition, from its service to Great Britain in the French and Indian Wars and its role in the Revolution to its part in the defense of the United States and other Allied nations in more recent conflicts. The Pennsylvania Military Museum is devoted to the state's military history and Stackpole Books is pleased to continue its collaboration with the Pennsylvania Historical and Museum Commission (PHMC) to feature the museum in this new volume of the Pennsylvania Trail of History Guides.

Each book in the series focuses on one of the historic sites or museums administered by the PHMC. The series was conceived and created by Stackpole Books with the cooperation of the PHMC's Division of Publications and Bureau of Historic Sites and Museums. Donna Williams heads the latter, and she and her staff of professionals review the text of each guidebook for accuracy and have made many valuable recommendations. Diane Reed, Chief of Publications, has facilitated relations between the PHMC and Stackpole from the project's inception, organized the review process with the commission, and attended to numerous details related to the venture.

At the Pennsylvania Military Museum, Director William Leach met with the authors and me to develop the scope and content of the guidebook. Museum Educator Joseph Horvath made integral contributions in the manuscript review process and devoted many hours to assisting me in selecting illustrations.

Arthur and Marjorie Miller, the authors of the text, are noted travel writers and authors of the comprehensive volume, *Pennsylvania Battlefields and Military Landmarks*. They bring an acute knowledge of the subject to this volume in a concise overview of Pennsylvania's military history, a profile of the Boal Troop and the shrine that led to the development of the museum, and a brief tour of the site.

Kyle R. Weaver, Editor
Stackpole Books

4

Introduction to the Site

The Pennsylvania Military Museum honors the contributions the commonwealth's soldiers, sailors, airmen, and marines have made to the defense of the state and the nation for more than two hundred years. There visitors find 18,000 square feet of exhibit space, a theater, galleries, and a gift shop inside the museum; military armaments and vehicles displayed on the sixty-seven-acre parklike grounds; and the 28th Infantry Division Shrine commemorating those who have fallen during the division's combat history.

Through exhibits, films, and programs, the museum is dedicated to Pennsylvania's military units, displays the uniforms and equipment of the common soldier and sailor, and provides brief summaries of the historical background of examples of military service. Displays of vehicles, firearms, uniforms, and photographs trace the state's military history. Interpretive exhibits concentrate on the individual serviceman and the role he or she played in conflicts in which Pennsylvanians were involved. The site is designed to broaden the public's understanding of how the state militia developed, its evolution into the Pennsylvania National Guard, and the organization of the 28th Division during World War I. Visitors learn how the National Guard stands ready to go into action in the event of a state emergency and as a standby defense force for the federal government. Other exhibits demonstrate how medical, technological, and scientific advancements initiated by the military have been adapted to improve the nation's general welfare. The museum staff is assisted by the Friends of the Pennsylvania Military Museum, a volunteer support group.

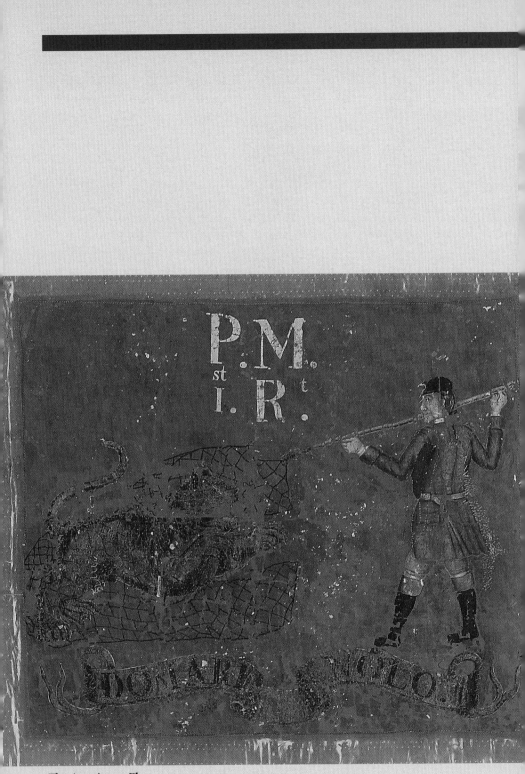

The Associators Flag. PENNSYLVANIA HISTORICAL AND MUSEUM COMMISSION

Pennsylvanians at Arms

Founded in 1681 upon William Penn's principles of tolerance and pacifism, the Pennsylvania proprietary colony did not field a state militia of any size throughout its first sixty-five years, although in 1740, Gov. George Thomas on his own authority raised seven hundred soldiers to fight for England against the Spanish in the Caribbean.

In 1747, with England and France at war with each other, French privateers sailed into Chesapeake Bay and up the Delaware River to threaten defenseless Philadelphia. Exasperated by the failure of efforts to get the Quaker-dominated Pennsylvania Assembly to authorize a compulsory service militia, as other colonies had done, Benjamin Franklin led a civic campaign to warn the city of the impending danger and organize a volunteer defense force, which he called "the Associators." Each member was to provide his own musket and ammunition and stand ready to be called out to defend the city at a moment's notice. In answer to Franklin's appeal at a public meeting, five hundred signed up that first night, and within weeks, one hundred companies had been formed within the province.

FRENCH AND INDIAN WAR

Such were the first efforts of Pennsylvania's citizen-soldiers to defend their colony. During the French and Indian War (1755–63), Pennsylvania territory needed to be defended along both the Delaware River and the frontier of the colony. In spite of the reluctance of Quaker members of the Assembly, militia laws were passed in November 1755 and March 1757 to provide troops to help defend the frontier settlers from increasing Indian attacks. The passage of the 1757 Militia Act brought about a turnover in power within Pennsylvania's General Assembly, ending what had long been a Quaker-imposed deadlock on militia and defense appropriations.

These newly authorized troops, together with the Associators, undertook responsibility for manning a chain of forts that were being built along the Allegheny Mountains. To supplement the garrisons at these frontier forts, the Assembly went a step further, authorizing a Pennsylvania Provincial Regiment of full-time paid soldiers. To spur the construction of the forts and better organize the town defenses against the Indian raids, the governor of the province sent out a commission that included Benjamin Franklin.

In 1756, a French and Delaware Indian force captured one of these frontier forts. In retaliation, Pennsylvanian lieutenant colonel John Armstrong and a task force of provincial soldiers took offensive action, destroying the Delaware village of Kittanning and liberating eleven prisoners. After the 1758 capture by a British-led force of the French stronghold of Fort Duquesne, located at the place where the Allegheny and Monongahela Rivers form the Ohio River, French influence largely disappeared from the Ohio River Valley.

Anthony Wayne. A native of Chester County, Pennsylvania, the general led Continental forces on his home ground in the Revolutionary War battles of Brandywine, Paoli, and Germantown. His portrait from the late 1790s is attributed to James Sharples Sr.
INDEPENDENCE NATIONAL HISTORICAL PARK

THE REVOLUTIONARY WAR

The concept of volunteer Associators continued under Pennsylvania's provincial government until the Revolutionary War completely changed the political landscape. In the resulting turmoil, the new state of Pennsylvania challenged British domination and dissolved its remaining ties to the Penn family's proprietary colony. The Pennsylvania constitution of 1776 created a new General Assembly and did away with the Associators. In their place, the Assembly the next year established a state militia, requiring military service for all white males able to bear arms. During the Revolutionary War, these militiamen, many of them former Associators, fought alongside soldiers of the regular Continental Army.

Valley Forge. Edwin Austin Abbey (1852–1911) commemorated the Continental Army's winter encampment in Pennsylvania in his 1910 painting Camp of the American Army at Valley Forge, February 1778, *depicting Prussian officer Baron Friedrich Wilhelm Augustus von Steuben training George Washington's troops.* BRIAN HUNT/PENNSYLVANIA CAPITOL PRESERVATION COMMITTEE

Meanwhile, in November 1775, the Continental Congress had authorized raising two battalions of marines to serve as guards aboard ships. Capt. Samuel Nicholas, the first commandant of Continental Marines, set up headquarters at the Tun Tavern in Philadelphia, where he recruited the first U.S. Marines with the help of the tavern proprietor, who received a commission as a captain.

Pennsylvanians in the national Continental Army took part in almost all the campaigns of the Revolution. The first unit raised by Congress in the fall of 1775 was Thompson's Rifle Battalion. After fighting bravely in the ill-fated Canadian Campaign of 1776, the battalion participated in the siege of Boston in 1775 and 1776 and the New York and New Jersey campaigns. The British thought that the capital of Philadelphia was of key importance and, in the summer of 1777, invaded and captured the city. The Battles of Brandywine, Paoli, and Germantown and theWhitemarsh skirmishes were fought on Pennsylvania soil during this time.

Following these battles, Gen. George Washington and his men went into winter quarters at Valley Forge, where they remained through the winter of 1777–78. During this period, Benjamin Franklin helped negotiate a new and vital alliance with France. In the spring of 1778, the British Army abandoned Philadelphia and moved to New York with the Continental Army in pursuit. The Pennsylvania frontier suffered heavily from British and Indian raids, until these attacks were answered in 1779 by expeditions led by John Sullivan and Daniel Brodhead against the Iroquois Confederacy. Altogether, Pennsylvania contributed an estimated 120,000 troops to the War of Independence, one-fourth of all those who fought on the patriot side.

Pennsylvania farm products and mineral resources were as essential as manpower to the success of the Revolutionary armies. A Pennsylvania member of the Continental Congress, Daniel Roberdeau, and a work crew extracted 2,000 pounds of lead from a mine near Altoona and used this metal to produce bullets for the Continental Army. At Carlisle, a Continental ordnance arsenal named Washingtonburgh (now Carlisle Barracks) turned out cannon and other munitions and the state actively encouraged the manufacture of the gunpowder the soldiers needed.

THE WAR OF 1812

Between 1803 and 1812, ongoing warfare in Europe between France and England was directly affecting American trade, as more than 1,500 U.S. vessels were seized. The Americans were growing increasingly angry over British attacks on their ships, which prevented their cargoes from reaching France. The resentment intensified because the British were also impressing American sailors into the Royal Navy. Furthermore, many Americans wanted to push the British out of the Great Lakes region, where they remained in violation of the

Lake Erie. In his 1873 painting The Battle of Lake Erie, *William Henry Powell (1823–79) rendered the most dramatic moment of the engagement—Perry's transfer from the battered* Lawrence *to the* Niagara *during heavy fire.* U.S. SENATE COLLECTION

treaty that ended the Revolutionary War. Some radicals in the United States even hoped to evict the British from Canada entirely, thus gaining control of all of northern North America. So, scarcely forty years after the Revolutionary War victory, the United States went to war with Britain again.

To counter a British sailing fleet that controlled Lake Erie, the Americans, under the leadership of Oliver Hazard Perry and native Pennsylvanian Daniel Dobbins, hurriedly built six new warships at Erie. In a blazing sea battle on Lake Erie on September 10, 1813, Perry defeated the British fleet. Perry was the only naval officer in U.S. history to defeat an entire British squadron and successfully bring back every enemy ship to his base as a prize of war. After more than two years of futile conflict, the peace talks brought the war to an end and gave the United States control of the Midwest, clearing the way for Americans who dreamed of settling in this region. Today a reconstruction of the Brig *Niagara* is on exhibit most days at the Erie Maritime Museum. The fully operational sailing ship, with its crew of forty, takes part in a schedule of sailing events each year on the Atlantic coast and in the Great Lakes region.

THE CIVIL WAR

Pennsylvania played an important role in preserving the Union during the Civil War. Nearly 350,000 Pennsylvanians served in the Union forces, including 8,600 African Americans, and the strong output of Pennsylvania industry added greatly to the economic and military superiority of the North.

Several Pennsylvanians are well known for the major roles they played in the war. Army leaders from the Keystone State included Generals George B.

George B. McClellan, born in Philadelphia, served as commander of the Army of the Potomac from August 1861 to November 1862 and commander in chief of the Union Army from November 1861 to March 1862.
LIBRARY OF CONGRESS

McClellan, George G. Meade, John F. Reynolds, Winfield Scott Hancock, and John F. Hartranft. In addition, Adm. David D. Porter opened the Mississippi River, and Rear Adm. John A. Dahlgren produced innovations in ordnance that greatly improved naval firepower.

The Confederates invaded Pennsylvania three times. In October 1862, following the Battle of Antietam, a Con-

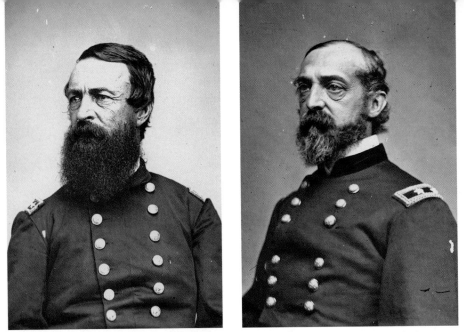

Above left: **David D. Porter**, *hero of New Orleans and Vicksburg, was a native of Chester, Pennsylvania. Above right:* **George G. Meade**. *The Pennsylvania general was the victor of the Battle of Gettysburg and commander of the Army of the Potomac through the second half of the war.* LIBRARY OF CONGRESS (BOTH)

Officers of the 4th Pennsylvania Cavalry *pose for photographer Alexander Gardner (1821–82) in Westover Landing, Virginia, at the close of the Peninsula Campaign in August 1862.* LIBRARY OF CONGRESS

Gettysburg. *The pivotal battle of the Civil War was fought in three bloody days in south-central Pennsylvania.* LIBRARY OF CONGRESS

federate cavalry force captured much-needed livestock, food, and ammunition at Chambersburg. In June 1863, the Confederates swept through Chambersburg once more, as Lee's army invaded the North in an offensive aimed at capturing the Pennsylvania capital of Harrisburg. This drive culminated in the decisive Battle of Gettysburg. At the end of the bitterly fought three-day battle, Union forces under General Meade succeeded in throwing back the Southern forces under Gen. Robert E. Lee, a major turning point in the struggle to save the Union. One-third of the troops who repelled this farthest Confederate advance into the North were Pennsylvanians.

A year later, in July 1864, a Confederate cavalry force attacked Chambersburg once again, demanding $500,000 ransom from the town. When the townspeople could not comply, the Confederates set fires that destroyed some three hundred dwellings, shops, and buildings.

After the Civil War, in 1870, at the urging of Gov. John W. Geary and Adj. Gen. John F. Hartranft, the commonwealth's legislature established the National Guard of Pennsylvania. This integrated the scattered militia companies into a single force, while, in 1878, the guard adopted a geographical division structure. The guard units in some cases were antecedents of the 28th Division units of World War I. National Guardsmen were called out as strikebreakers in 1875, to protect company property during a strike in the anthracite coal region of northeastern Pennsylvania, and again in 1892, during a violent strike at the Homestead Works of the Carnegie Steel Company near Pittsburgh.

SPANISH-AMERICAN WAR.

In 1898, the United States went to war with Spain over remnants of the Spanish empire in the Caribbean and the Philippines. Although no Pennsylvania units fought in the main battleground of Cuba, a regiment from the Keystone State participated in the occupation of Puerto Rico. Another regiment, the 10th Pennsylvania Volunteers, was one of the first American military units to engage in land combat in the Philippine Islands, during part of the ensuing Filipino Insurrection. Other Pennsylvanians participated in the naval victory of Santiago Bay, which rendered the Spanish position in Cuba untenable.

Numerous Pennsylvanians also served on the ships of Adm. George Dewey's battle fleet, which bottled up and obliterated the Spanish fleet in Manila harbor. Steaming into the harbor under cover of darkness on May 1, 1898, Dewey's fleet found eight Spanish warships lined up at one end of the bay. The U.S. warships turned parallel to the line of Spanish ships and opened fire, with telling effect. Five times the U.S. ships moved past the Spanish "sitting ducks," causing explosions and starting fires. So one-sided was the Battle of Manila Bay that Dewey ordered his men to take time for breakfast, then go back into action to finish off the Spanish ships and bombard a nearby arsenal. By noon, not a single ship in the Spanish fleet remained afloat. Dewey's flagship, the USS *Olympia*, was hit seven or eight times, but no one on board was killed. Today the USS *Olympia*, preserved as the last remaining U.S. warship of the Spanish-American War, is open to visitors at its berth in Philadelphia, part of the Independence Seaport Museum on the Delaware River waterfront.

THE FILIPINO
INSURRECTION

In the Philippines, the 10th Regiment of Pennsylvania Volunteers and other U.S. Army units went into combat to enforce the political decisions that resulted from the U.S. defeat of Spain in the Spanish-American War.

In May 1898, scarcely a week after the United States had declared war on Spain, Adm. George Dewey and U.S. Navy warships bottled up and destroyed part of the Spanish fleet in Manila harbor, and U.S. Army forces seized the capital of Manila. Dewey had encouraged the Filipino population and Gen. Emilio Aguinaldo, the head of the Philippine government in exile, to rise up against their Spanish rulers, and after this defeat, Aguinaldo declared that the Philippines were now independent from Spain and were a republic.

But in the treaty with the United States that ended the war, although Spain "relinquished all claims" to Cuba, to which the United States had already agreed to grant independence, it "ceded" ownership of Puerto Rico, Guam, and the Philippines to the United States. Aguinaldo, who had led an earlier insurrection against the Spanish in 1896–97 and allied his troops with the Americans, felt betrayed, insisting that the Philippines should be a sovereign nation.

When President William McKinley made it clear that the Philippines would not be granted independence, fighting broke out on February 4, 1899, on the main island of Luzon. To oppose the insurgency, the U.S. Army had 21,000 soldiers, later reinforced to more than 100,000, against 30,000 Filipino troops. The 10th Pennsylvania joined the attack as U.S. forces pushed the insurgents out of Manila to the north. Navy warships pounded the rebel positions from the sea, and the smoke of fires and battle hung over the capital.

After suffering several defeats in trench fighting, Aguinaldo's forces resorted to guerrilla warfare, employing hit-and-run attacks to cut U.S. lines of communication, impede railway shipments of supplies, and ambush U.S. soldiers in an attempt to undermine their determination and force them to withdraw. Unsure which Filipinos were civilians and which were combatants, Army soldiers killed a number of civilians, and both sides tortured prisoners. The official War Department record of the war later concluded that the insurgent foes were "clever, courageous and unremitting." The campaign waged under Gen. Arthur McArthur is considered a classic anti-insurgent action. The challenge of surviving in the jungle was so extreme that few soldiers who fought there were still in the Army by World War I.

By February 1901, after two years of combat, Aguinaldo had retreated to a village in northeast Luzon. When one of Aguinaldo's lieutenants was captured, he disclosed the location of the rebel chieftain. Posing as captives taken by other Filipino fighters, American soldiers entered the village. They captured Aguinaldo after a brief skirmish and took him to Manila. From his jail cell, the insurgent leader later issued a message to his generals directing them to submit to U.S. authority and end the bloodshed.

On July 4, 1902, President Theodore Roosevelt declared the insurrection at an end. The fighting had cost the U.S. Army 3,493 men killed and 2,828 wounded. Filipino casualties were estimated to be 20,000 combatants killed or wounded, as well as some 200,000 civilians, who died mostly from disease or starvation.

Years later, in 1935, the Philippines became a self-governing commonwealth. On July 4, 1946, after being liberated from Japanese occupation in World War II by the American armed forces, under the son of Arthur McArthur, Douglas, the Philippines gained independence.

Spanish-American War. The National Guard of Pennsylvania trained for the war at Camp Thomas in Chickamauga, Georgia. The colorful mess section of Company G, 1st Regiment, was captured in this 1898 photograph. PENNSYLVANIA NATIONAL GUARD MUSEUM, FORT INDIANTOWN GAP

WORLD WAR I

When World War I erupted in 1914 and spread throughout Europe, most Americans opposed becoming involved in the war. In line with the sentiment of his countrymen, President Woodrow Wilson declared the United States to be a neutral nation and asked that other countries not interfere with its ships as they continued their normal trade routes to Europe.

But German U-boat submarines, in their endeavor to blockade supplies coming by sea to its enemy the United Kingdom, soon began to sink neutral ships as well. In May 1915, without warning, a U-boat torpedoed and sank the British passenger liner *Lusitania* off the coast of Ireland. Among the 1,201 passengers who died when the ship went down were 128 Americans.

This inflamed public opinion, as did other provocations that followed, including German efforts to involve the United States in a war with Mexico. In 1916, Mexico's troubles spilled over the United States border. To keep the peace, Pennsylvania's National Guard was federalized. The training and experience of the "Border" prepared the division for World War I service.

On April 6, 1917, Congress declared war on Germany. Responding to anguished entreaties from the Allied forces, which had suffered tremendous casualties, the United States now began to send its soldiers to support the British and French troops on the battlefield in

PATRIOTISM AND SUSPICION

When the United States entered World War I, the civil rights of some citizens were occasionally swept away by the flood tide of American patriotic fervor. After Congress declared war on April 6, 1917, all the pacifists—and there had been many—seemed to fade away as a red, white, and blue Americanism took over.

The first to be caught up in this crusade for Americanism were citizens of German extraction. Gov. James M. Cox of Ohio, the Democratic presidential nominee in 1920, urged the Ohio legislature to forbid the instruction of German in elementary schools, calling it part of a German plot to gain the loyalty of American schoolchildren. Communities burned books about Germany, and an Ohio school board sold German publications to a wastepaper company.

Even German terms were exorcised from everyday language. Hamburger became "liberty steak," and sauerkraut was called "liberty cabbage." The names of streets and schools that sounded German were anglicized.

Musicians were undecided about what music to play. Ernestine Schumann-Heink, world famous Austrian contralto, with sons in both the German and U.S. armies, was forced to remove German songs from her repertoire. Leopold Stokowski, conductor of the Philadelphia Orchestra, wrote to President Woodrow Wilson that he would cease to play music by German and Austrian composers, although he felt that music by Bach, Beethoven, Mozart, and Brahms should not be considered the exclusive possession of German-speaking nations and therefore would continue to be played.

Wilson used the power of the federal government, invoking the Alien Enemies Act of 1798, which gave him the authority to imprison enemy aliens without a trial. During the first year of U.S. involvement, government agents arrested 1,200 German aliens. The act even served as the justification to arrest members of the Socialist Party. Another wartime law, the Sedition Act of 1918, forbade "uttering, printing, writing, or publishing any disloyal, profane, scurrilous, or abusive language" about the U.S. government, Army, or Navy.

France. These men had borne the brunt of the fighting, which had evolved into a stalemate of punishing trench warfare. By June 1917, the first 15,000 U.S. soldiers, under the command of Gen. John J. Pershing, had disembarked in France; by October, the first troops had moved to the front to support the beleaguered French forces.

As part of this military buildup, the 28th Infantry Division was created at Camp Hancock, Georgia, from Pennsylvania National Guard units. Federalized as part of the U.S. Army, the 28th arrived in France in May 1918, just in time to join the hard-pressed French forces in opposing the last major German offensive of the war, along the Marne River near the border between France and Belgium.

The weakened French forces had given way before a superior German attack, and the government was making plans to evacuate from Paris, only fifty miles from the front. Coming under heavy fire from several German units, four rifle companies of the 28th's 109th Infantry Regiment that had been integrated into a French unit were cut off when the French soldiers retreated without warning. Of the more than 500 men of the 28th who entered the battle, only 150 were left at the end of the fighting. The Germans then continued

Bayonet Drill *of the 28th Division, circa 1918, at Camp Hancock, Georgia.* LIBRARY OF CONGRESS

to push their way toward the main Allied defense line. Here the combined forces of the American Army, U.S. Marines, and British and French troops were finally able to halt the German advance. General Pershing called this Second Battle of the Marne "the Gettysburg of this war" and the turning point of the conflict.

In September, the Allied forces responded with a major offensive of their own, crossing the Marne and recapturing all the terrain the Germans had taken in their earlier offensive. Over the next two months, thousands of U.S. "doughboys," including Pennsylvanians, pushed the Germans steadily back with battles at St. Mihiel and in the Meuse-Argonne region. In November, with the German Army disintegrating, Germany's leader, Kaiser Wilhelm, fled his country. A defeated Germany agreed to an armistice on the victor's terms, which brought the punishing fighting to an end. Finally, on November 11, 1918, all became quiet on the western front.

Throughout the war, Pennsylvania's mills and factories had provided a large share of the weapons and materiel needed to support the troops in Europe, including the large Midvale Steel and Eddystone Ridge factories, both near Philadelphia. To quickly build the cargo ships needed to transport men and equipment to Europe, the U.S. government financed several shipyards. The largest of these was the Hog Island Ship Yard on the Delaware River in Philadelphia. Here a workforce that reached 30,000 produced 122 Hog Island–class freighters in three years, using fifty building ways. A smaller shipyard at nearby Bristol delivered another forty ships. According to legend, it was the Hog Island yard that gave its name to that favorite Philadelphia sandwich, the "Hoagie."

Nearly 3,000 separate firms fulfilled contracts for war supplies. Pennsylvanians subscribed to nearly $3 billion worth of Liberty and Victory bonds, and 370,000 Pennsylvanians saw duty in the military services.

African Americans in World War I

At the start of World War I, the United States had a professional Army of only about 128,000 men. Once in the conflict, the country's armed forces were rapidly expanded through both voluntary enlistments and a draft that required all men between ages twenty-one and thirty (later expanded to eighteen through forty-five) to register for military service. By the end of the war, the U.S. armed forces had grown to almost 5 million men and women, of which half had been drafted.

To meet the number of soldiers required, African Americans were needed, and the Army drafted them along with white citizens. But the mobilization of black soldiers showed a pattern of discrimination in their selection, training, assignment, and leadership policies, reflecting attitudes then common in much of the country. During this war "to make the world safe for democracy," the nation's 12 million black citizens remained near the bottom of the nation's economic and social ladder. Black men were frequently recruited despite illnesses and other disabilities that would have exempted their white counterparts from service. At a time when the Army was seeking doctors and dentists, black men in these professions were turned down for commissions, even though they were later drafted as privates.

Many of the training camps were in the South, where African Americans were quartered in segregated areas. Generally the clothing, housing, feeding, and working conditions of the black troops were inferior to those offered white soldiers. Shelter for black troops often consisted of tents without the flooring or boxing usually provided for others, and sometimes the shelters had no stoves for heat in the winter.

From the beginning, the Army assigned most of the black soldiers to stevedore regiments and labor battalions. They worked on the docks; cleaned up the camps; hauled coal, wood, and stone; dug ditches; took care of livestock; and disposed of garbage. In some cases,

TRENCH WARFARE

Four months after the beginning of Germany's 1914 invasion of Belgium and France, the war had turned into a deadlock between the combatants along the western front. World War I was characterized by the predominance of defensive weapons over those that were necessary to conduct a breakthrough offense. The machine gun, mortar, and improved artillery created a stalemate that neither side could turn into a war of movement. The battlefront at that point extended 470 miles across the flat terrain of Belgium and northeastern France, to the border with Switzerland. The soldiers on both sides dug in, creating systems of trenches at or below ground level, where they could protect themselves and their equipment and supplies from artillery and high explosives that could rain down on them. Digging trenches for protection on the battlefield was not new, but in World War I, the soldiers were forced to live in their trenches for months. This static style of trench warfare continued for the next three years, with neither side succeeding in advancing more than a few miles from its line of trenches.

Such *front-line trenches* were usually dug seven feet deep and about six feet wide, just spacious enough for two soldiers to pass. The trenches were excavated in a zigzag pattern so that no enemy sniper could shoot straight down a trench at the soldiers located there. Sandbags filled with earth were piled along the forward edge of the trench as additional protection against enemy bullets. A *fire step* was cut into the trench on the side facing the enemy, allowing soldiers to step up and take a firing position to repel any attack that approached over *no-man's-land*, the field of conflict that lay between the opposing trenches. Round-the-clock sentries stood on the fire step when on watch, and the whole unit stood on it when "standing to," on the alert for a possible enemy attack.

The no-man's-land between trenches soon became a wasteland of craters, blackened tree stumps, and an occasional shell of a building. This contested area between the opposing trench lines was about 250 yards wide, but it varied from only 7 yards at one location to some 500 yards at another.

Behind the front-line trenches ran *support trenches*, where off-duty soldiers lived in dugouts they carved out of the walls. Replacement troops and supplies moved up to the battlefront through a network of *communications trenches*, depressed roadways that connected the support trenches to the rear area. The wounded moved through these trenches in the opposite direction, to the medical stations in the rear. The cannons and mortars of the field artillery were set up behind the support trenches.

Life in the trenches was miserable. The smell of dead bodies and human waste lingered in the air. Rats, which sometimes grew to the size of a cat, were a constant problem, spreading infection and contaminating the food. Getting food to those manning the trenches also was difficult. Food prepared in field kitchens behind the lines was carried through the trenches to the front in cooking pots, reused gas cans, or large jars. By the time it reached the fighting men up front, it was invariably cold. The bulk of the men's diet was bully beef (canned corned beef), bread, and biscuits. Both bread and biscuits were usually stale by the time they reached the troops.

The soldiers in the trenches had trouble keeping themselves dry, especially in the waterlogged areas of Belgium, where the land lay only a few feet above sea level. During a rainfall, water filled the trenches and had to be pumped out afterward. Frogs, slugs, and horned beetles thrived in the damp soil. Lice got into soldiers' uniforms and transmitted trench fever, an illness that generated a high fever and pain in the joints, bones, and muscles.

Front-line trench duty was dangerous. Almost every day, enemy shells exploded over the trenches. It was later estimated that one-third of all the soldiers who became casualties on the western front were killed or wounded while supposedly protected in the trenches.

Trench Warfare in World War I. PENNSYLVANIA STATE ARCHIVES

Troops generally served in a front-line trench for a few days to a week, followed by another week in a support trench. Then they were rotated to the rear, where they were held in reserve, although still ready to repel an attack if called upon. In the course of a year in the trenches, a soldier spent an average of 70 days in a front-line trench, another 30 days in a nearby support trench, and 120 days in reserve. If he was lucky, the weary combatant might then be granted about two weeks of leave, often his only leave break in a year of battle duty. The weapons to change trench warfare were invented or improved by the end of the war. They included the tank, the sub-machine gun, and the airplane. All figured prominently in a very different kind of war.

Although soldiers have continued to dig in under fire, advanced land weapons, improved armored vehicles, and devastating air attacks have made trench warfare obsolete.

African Americans soldiers from Philadelphia during World War I.

they were trained for more technical positions, such as mechanics or drivers.

Once they got to France, the black stevedores packed and unpacked the American Expeditionary Force. On a single day at one port, the stevedores brought to shore 42,000 men with their portable gear and unloaded 5,000 tons of cargo. Sometimes they worked in shifts, and sometimes for sixteen-hour stretches. A group in Brest unloaded 1,200 tons of flour in nine and a half hours, and then, in an effort to break their own record, averaged 2,000 tons a day for five more days.

Black laborers were also responsible for building warehouses, sheds, and supply dumps near ports and at related railroad facilities. They built barracks at the bases and constructed temporary housing as the combat troops moved toward the front.

There were, however, two African American fighting organizations: the 92nd Division and 93rd Division (Provisional). The 92nd was composed entirely of soldiers who had been drafted. The 93rd was made up of three infantry regiments drawn from National Guard units and a fourth regiment of black draftees. It was termed provisional because it never reached full strength. A few African American officers were selected for these black divisions, but most of their officers were white. Both divisions saw battle action, and despite a lack of basic training, both performed creditably.

When they returned home after the armistice, the black troops were treated with respect in the large Northern cities, if not enthusiasm. In rural areas, especially in the South, they were sometimes met with hostility.

Women in World War I

During World War I, as the United States shipped hundreds of thousands of men overseas for military duty, women were eager and willing to fill the vacancies the men left behind in factories and offices. Unlike many European countries, which quickly recognized the wisdom of using womanpower, the U.S. military was reluctant to accept the services of women, despite the obvious need.

The U.S. Navy was the exception and recruited 11,000 women to serve as yeomen over the course of the war. Secretary of the Navy Josephus Daniels surprised the naval service when he issued an order to enroll women in the ranks as yeomen. There were few requirements: A woman had to be between the ages of eighteen and thirty-five, of good character, and neat in appearance. The Navy preferred high school graduates with business or office experience but did not require a college education. The prospective yeoman simply had to present herself at a recruiting station, be interviewed for qualifications, and fill out the application forms. After she passed a physical examination, she was sworn in and signed up for a four-year enlistment. The women performed clerical and bookkeeping duties in the bureaus in Washington, D.C., at Navy yards, in all naval districts, and at numerous shore stations.

The Marine Corps was not as quick as the Navy to turn to women for help, but heavy fighting and mounting casualties in France during the summer of 1918 changed some minds, and the Marines began recruiting women that August. The idea appealed to many women in the civilian workforce. In New York City alone, 2,000 hopeful applicants lined up at the recruiting office in response to a newspaper article announcing that the Marine Corps was looking for "intelligent young women." The recruiting sergeant in Philadelphia also had a large response from local advertisements.

"Free a Man to Fight" became the Marines' slogan, and it proved to be a valid phrase. As fast as men could be spared from Marine Corps offices in the United States, they were sent to join Marine units in France. All female recruits were enrolled as privates in the Marine Corps Reserve for a period of four years. Their pay was the same as for the men, and they received an additional $83.40 a month for subsistence and quarters because no barracks were provided for the women.

Several thousand skilled and patriotic U.S. nurses went to France in 1917–18 to tend the sick and wounded of the American Expeditionary Forces. More than 12,000 nurses were on active duty in the Army Nurse Corps in June 1918, with 5,350 serving overseas. But still more were needed. As part of the general preparedness movement before the United States entered the war, the American Red Cross agreed to supplement the Army's medical teams with complete hospital units that would be ready for possible transfer to the government in case of emergency. During 1916, many of the civilian hospitals throughout the country, including one in Philadelphia, organized such units. The hospital units were set up with the concurrence of the Army's surgeon general and the financial aid of the local chapters of the Red Cross. The Red Cross also organized and maintained a register of qualified nurses available for service in time of war.

This advance planning paid off, as these stateside hospital units were transferred to France to staff the base hospitals that formed the primary treatment centers for soldiers wounded in the field. The doctors and nurses in these units, working long hours under difficult conditions, treated a steady flow of men with shrapnel wounds, mustard gas burns, respiratory problems from phosgene gas inhalation, infected wounds, battlefield trauma, and other injuries and afflictions.

Other women served with—but not in—the Army as field clerks, or in organizations, such as the Red Cross, Salvation Army, YMCA, and the Jewish Welfare Board. By war's end, more than 40,000 women had proudly served their country. They worked as physicians, bilingual telephone operators, physical and occupational therapists called reconstruction aides, and recreational workers in canteens organized behind the lines.

WORLD WAR II

Two decades later, the December 7, 1941, Japanese attack on Pearl Harbor propelled the United States into World War II. The country now joined the Allies against Germany and Italy in Europe while simultaneously battling the Japanese in the Pacific.

The Keystone State played a vital role, with more than 1.5 million Pennsylvanians serving in the Army, Navy, Marine Corps, and Air Corps. Pennsylvania supplied one out of every seven men in the armed forces, as well as more than 20,000 women, who served in all theaters of the war. Although New York mobilized more personnel, the Keystone State lost more servicemen than any other state, 33,000 in all. Thirty-five Pennsylvanians earned the Medal of Honor, the highest honor the country can bestow on a combatant.

Several top military commanders of the war were from the state, including Gen. George C. Marshall of Uniontown, who was chief of staff of the Army; Gen. Henry (Hap) Arnold of Gladwyne, who commanded the Army Air Corps; Adm. Harold Stark of Wilkes-Barre, who commanded all naval operations in European waters; and Gen. Carl A. Spaatz

Medal of Honor awarded to Foster J. Sayers of Blanchard, Pennsylvania, during World War II. PENNSYLVANIA MILITARY MUSEUM

of Boyertown, who commanded the 8th Air Force in England. Pennsylvanians served with the 1st and 29th Divisions on Utah and Omaha Beaches on D-Day; with the Marines at Guadalcanal, Okinawa, and Iwo Jima; with the Navy at Leyte Gulf; and with the Army Air Corps over Berlin and Tokyo.

Indiantown Gap, the home of Pennsylvania's National Guard, was one of forty military installations in Pennsylvania and became a major training center for the soldiers headed for Europe.

In the early days of the war, the 28th Division was mobilized and ordered to guard vital shipyards, coal mines, and steel mills on the home front against possible German sabotage. After training at Camp Livingston, Louisiana, and in England for two years, the 28th partici-

George C. Marshall and Henry "Hap" Arnold. The chief of staff of the Army and commander of the Army Air Corps both hailed from Pennsylvania. NATIONAL ARCHIVES

Carl A. Spaatz, commander of the 8th Air Force in England, was a native of Boyertown, Pennsylvania. LIBRARY OF CONGRESS

Harold R. Stark, the admiral who commanded naval operations in Europe, was from Wilkes-Barre, Pennsylvania. LIBRARY OF CONGRESS

pated in the French Campaign. The division saw heavy fighting in France, starting on July 22, 1944. The 28th advanced from Normandy across western France, only to find itself in the thick of hedgerow fighting through towns such as Percy, Montbray, Montgouray, Gathemo, and St. Sever de Calvados by the end of July.

Crossing the Seine River, Allied forces including the 28th Division liberated Paris, the French capital, in August 1944. The 28th, chosen to provide a show of force in the city to discourage further enemy underground activity, undertook a tactical military maneuver to move the division's 15,000 men and their equipment through the city. As an extra benefit, the division joined in a victory parade down the Champs Élysées to the cheers of millions of grateful French citizens. No sooner was the parade concluded, however, than the soldiers shifted back to battle dress, took up defensive positions, and prepared to continue offensive operations against German forces northeast of Paris.

Even tougher fighting lay ahead. The advance continued northward toward Belgium and Luxembourg, crossing the Meuse River. During early September, the Pennsylvania troops were able to advance an average of seventeen miles a day against the weakening resistance of German battle groups as the division fanned out into Luxembourg. On September 11, the 28th Division became the first major American unit to cross

D-Day. *First Division Infantry storm Omaha Beach.* NATIONAL ARCHIVES

the German border. It marked the first time since the days of Napoleon that an opposing army breeched Germany's western border.

Pushing ahead, the 28th along with four other divisions met strong German opposition in November in the Huertgen Forest. The heavily wooded and mountainous area along the Germany-Belgium border formed part of the enemy's Siegfried Line, a system of fortified bunkers and gun emplacements that ringed Germany. Their usual air support and artillery were useless in this forested area, where the GIs were committed to fighting in almost perpetual gloom, in weather that alternated between sleet, snow, and rain, exposed to incessant enemy fire and without the possibility of changing into dry clothes. The Sherman tanks and supply trucks that were supposed to support the ground troops were unable to negotiate the narrow mountainside roads. When the soldiers tried to move forward, it was like "walking into hell," as one soldier described it. Even the crackle of pine needles underfoot could reveal a soldier's position to an enemy sharpshooter. From their concealed bunkers, the Germans sent forth a hail of machine-gun bullets, rifle fire, and mortar shells. Some GIs were caught in thick minefields. Despite the dreadful conditions, the Keystone soldiers remained on the line for fourteen days, capturing two towns, but then were overwhelmed by a German panzer tank counterattack. The Huertgen Forest Campaign was one of the most costly U.S. actions of World War II, and it cost the 28th and its attached units alone 6,184 casualties.

After the brutal fighting in the Huertgen Forest, the 28th Division was assigned to hold a twenty-five-mile sector of the line along the Our River in

Women's Auxiliary Army Corps (WAACs) stationed at the 3rd Army Air Force Base, Will Rogers Field, Oklahoma City, circa 1943. PENNSYLVANIA MILITARY MUSEUM

the Ardennes region of eastern Belgium and northern Luxembourg, supposedly a quiet sector of the front. Here what proved to be the final and largest German offensive of the war was thrown against the overextended and thinly held American line for five days. Called the Battle of the Bulge, this proved to be the biggest battle fought in American history, involving more than 1 million troops.

Even though the Germans achieved total surprise, nowhere did the American troops give ground to the vastly superior enemy force without a fight. The 28th prevented the enemy from immediately crossing the Our River, thus delaying and restricting the German advance. Within three days, the determined American stand and the arrival of powerful reinforcements ensured that the German attack would not achieve the objectives

the enemy had sought. All the Germans could achieve was to push out a "bulge" in the Allied line at a huge cost to them in casualties, tanks, and materiel. Four weeks later, after more grim fighting with heavy losses on both sides, the battlefront was pushed back and the bulge ceased to exist. The division's embattled defense of its position gave renewed emphasis to its nickname of "Bloody Bucket," a term given to it by German opponents in World War I for the shape of the Americans' shoulder patches. The names of 2,860 members of the 28th who died in these and other battles

are now engraved on the division's National World War II Shrine, which stands adjacent to the Pennsylvania Military Museum.

In the war in the Pacific, the United States had to fight its way back after the disastrous surprise attack by the Japanese on Pearl Harbor that crippled the U.S. fleet. The Japanese seemed on their way to conquering Southeast Asia. The course of the war was changed, however, through three dramatic turning points: the naval Battle of the Coral Sea (May 3–8, 1942); the air and sea Battle of Midway (June 4, 1942); and the con-

The Bantam Jeep became the standard mode of transportation during World War II. PENNSYLVANIA MILITARY MUSEUM

quest by land troops of Guadalcanal (August 1942 to February 1943). In the months that followed, the Japanese fleet and Air Force were virtually wiped out in a series of one-sided battles, U.S. submarines sank hundreds of enemy cargo ships, and long-range bombers destroyed large areas of cities on the Japanese mainland. When islands close to Japan—Iwo Jima and Okinawa—were seized, the Japanese turned to suicidal kamikaze attacks against U.S. ships. An invasion of Japan was planned but became unnecessary when the world's first atomic bombs were dropped on Hiroshima and Nagasaki in August 1945. Japan surrendered unconditionally, ending the war in the Pacific.

On the home front, Pennsylvania again contributed mightily to providing the fighting men overseas with the arms and equipment they needed. Its steel mills produced one-third of all the U.S. steel used during the war, and it was the third-largest producer of guns and ammunition and sixth in total war production. The state generated more than $13 billion in war materiels as many women replaced male workers in the factories. Berwick's American Car and Foundry turned out as many as thirty-six M3 light battlefield tanks a day. Bantam Car Company of Butler designed and produced what it called the Bantam Reconnaissance Vehicle (BRV), commonly known as the jeep. This small company manufactured more than 2,600 jeeps, and the basic design it had developed was maintained even after contracts went to larger manufacturers, which increased production to 600,000 vehicles.

To do their part for the war effort, Pennsylvanians planted victory gardens, endured gas and food rationing, and pitched in with scrap drives and salvage collections. Millions of backyards and rooftops sprouted the wartime vegetable gardens.

THE KOREAN AND VIETNAM WARS

After World War II, the United Nations was established as a parliament of governments in the hope that disputes between nations could be settled peacefully. Nevertheless, a Cold War and an arms race began between Communist countries and the U.S., resulting in several undeclared and limited conflicts. Between 1950 and 1953, Pennsylvanians were among the many Americans in the armed forces who fought with the South Koreans against the North Koreans and their Chinese allies in the Korean War.

Korea was one of the first conflicts of the decades long Cold War with Communist nations. NATIONAL ARCHIVES

Vietnam*. A wounded PFC from Pennsylvania receives treatment during
Operation Hue City in 1968.* NATIONAL ARCHIVES

Pennsylvania's 28th Division was one of
four National Guard divisions called to
active duty during this crisis, and it was
deployed to Germany to help deflect
possible aggression by the Soviet Union
or its allies during the Cold War period.
Another Pennsylvania reserve unit that
fought in Korea was the 213th antiair-
craft unit from Lehigh County.

The United States entered the
Korean War at the request of the United
Nations, responding to the invasion of
South Korea by the Communist forces
of North Korea. In the first months, the
South Korean Army was pushed to the
southern tip of the Korean Peninsula,
where Allied troops reinforced the South
Koreans and halted the enemy offensive.
U.S. forces then successfully executed a
risky amphibious landing at the port of
Inchon, on the west coast of the penin-
sula, thus outflanking the North Korean
forces and capturing the capital city of
Seoul. Allied land offensives attacking
from the south and west caught the
North Koreans in a pincer movement,
capturing or destroying most of their

army. When the Allied forces continued
to push northward on the peninsula, the
Communist forces of China entered the
conflict in November 1950, engaging
U.S. Marines and U.S. Army troops in
fierce fighting. Continued battle action
resulted in a stalemate on the battlefield
and led to an armistice that officially
divided the peninsula into North Korea
and South Korea.

Vietnam became another arena
of conflict. After widespread attacks by
the Viet Cong forces of North Vietnam
against South Vietnam during early
1965, President Lyndon Johnson
ordered the first large contingent of U.S.
troops to defend the embattled South
Vietnam. He also authorized the beginning of an air-bombing campaign,
which continued on and off until the
end of 1972. The United States rapidly
escalated its military involvement in
South Vietnam over the next two years,
and by 1967, 485,000 U.S. military personnel were in the theater. By 1971, with
U.S. troops changing their tactics from
an offensive to a defensive role, the Air

Force instituted a massive bombing campaign of the North Vietnamese capital of Hanoi and other targets. This eventually led to a negotiated peace agreement signed in Paris in 1973. The agreement called for a cease-fire and the withdrawal of all but a few U.S. troops from South Vietnam. Although the United States promised South Vietnam that it would provide the resources necessary to protect the country, the North Vietnamese renewed their offensive and marched into Saigon in April 1975, unifying the country under Communism. The war was the longest conflict fought by U.S. forces and is acknowledged to be their first military defeat. South Vietnam lost more than 1 million soldiers and citizens in the war, as did North Vietnam. During the conflict, 2.5 million Americans from the Army, Air Force, Navy, Marines, and Coast Guard served in South Vietnam, including many Pennsylvanians. The Vietnam Veterans Memorial in Washington, D.C., includes the names of 1,449 Pennsylvanians among the 58,715 who died as a result of combat in Vietnam.

RECENT CONFLICTS

After the termination of the military draft in 1973, many of Pennsylvania's sons and daughters continued to serve in the peacetime volunteer armed forces. By the 1980s, the tension of the Cold War was beginning to ease, and the country's military interests turned to humanitarian relief and peacekeeping, as evidenced by U.S. involvement in Lebanon, Grenada, Panama, Haiti, and Somalia. With the fall of the Berlin Wall and the disintegration of the Soviet Union in 1991, America found itself the sole superpower.

Eight Pennsylvania National Guard units were mobilized to join the Allied coalition in the 1990 invasion of Iraq, Operation Desert Storm, which turned back Iraq's aggression against neighboring Kuwait, liberating that small country and defeating the Iraqi army of Saddam Hussein. The Allied forces captured nearly 60,000 Iraqi prisoners. Pennsylvanians served on the Navy warships that pounded Iraq with missiles fired from the Arabian Gulf, while Air Force and Navy pilots bombed military targets. On February 15, 1991, thirteen members of the 14th Quartermaster Detachment from Greensburg were killed in an Iraqi missile attack on Dhahran, Saudi Arabia.

From 1996 to 2001, Army and Air National Guard units were deployed to Germany, Hungary, Croatia, Bosnia, and Kosovo in support of UN actions and to the former Yugoslavia as NATO peacekeepers.

Specialized units were ordered to Afghanistan as part of a military intervention in October 2001 by U.S. and Allied forces to defeat the Taliban regime, which harbored international terrorists who carried out attacks on the United States. From 2003 to 2005, more than 4,000 Pennsylvanian citizen-soldiers, marines, sailors, and airmen took part in the second invasion of Iraq and the occupation of that country, searching for weapons of mass destruction, providing convoy security, protecting officials, combating insurrectionists, and rebuilding facilities.

True to its dual nature as both a state and federal military armed force, the Pennsylvania National Guard also has responded to more than sixty orders from the governor in the last fifty years. Soldiers and airmen have reacted swiftly and heroically in times of state emergencies, saving lives and preserving order during blizzards, floods, riots, and labor strikes. As a National Guard force subject to mobilization into the U.S. Army in time

Persian Gulf, 1998. *David Dinardi, of Philadelphia, front, and other aviation ordnancemen aboard USS* George Washington *move MK-83 bombs during an operation to enforce a no-fly-zone over southern Iraq.* KRISTOFFER WHITE/U.S. DEPARTMENT OF DEFENSE

Relief. *The military also carries out humanitarian efforts in war-torn areas around the world. In this image from Bagram, Afghanistan, taken in October 2002, an Afghan man receives a box of clothing donated by the 339th Combat Support Hospital, Pittsburgh, Pennsylvania, at the 44th Task Force Combat Support Hospital.* STEVE FAULISI/U.S. DEPARTMENT OF DEFENSE

of emergency, the 28th Infantry Division today includes three fully mechanized infantry brigades, artillery, support command, a combat aviation brigade, a combat engineer brigade, and several separate battalions and company-size elements. It is one of the most deployed National Guard divisions in the nation, with soldiers serving in Afghanistan, Iraq, and on homeland security duty. The division now numbers 15,000 soldiers, who maintain a high state of readiness by training within 153 different units in armories in eighty-four cities and towns across the state.

Pennsylvanians—from the early militiamen to today's members of the U.S. Navy, Air Force, Marine Corps, and Army—have always been quick to respond to a call to arms to defend their state or their country. These Pennsylvanians know that the hard work of those back home in industry and agriculture will provide them with what they need while performing their duty, and that their friends and families in the Keystone State will also give them the moral support a fighting man or woman needs.

The Boal Troop and the History of the Museum

The Pennsylvania Military Museum owes its beginnings to a man who was first an architect, and then helped his country mobilize and prepare for World War I well before this nation agreed to support its European allies in the conflict. Raised in a wealthy family, Theodore Davis Boal studied architecture in Paris and married a French woman, Mathilde de Lagarde. In 1898, he returned to the United States with his wife and young son. He purchased a farm at Boalsburg that had long been in his family, turning it into a country estate.

When war broke out in Europe in 1914 between Britain, France, and Russia on one side and Austria-Hungary, Germany, and the Ottoman Empire on the other, Boal became a strong advocate of the Preparedness Movement in the United States, which called for universal military training of American men and their conscription into the armed forces. Early in 1915, two years before the United States entered the war, Boal and his son, Pierre, volunteered to serve with the French armed forces. The senior Boal became a quartermaster in a Belgian regiment; Pierre was first a member of the French cavalry and later a flier with the Lafayette Flying Corps, a group of American aviators who served in French uniform. Boal also donated money to French hospitals and organized several military canteens for European troops at Calais and along the front lines.

By the time he returned to the United States several months later, Boal had become convinced that America would soon find itself pulled into the war in Europe. In the spring of 1916, he laid the foundation for a horse-mounted machine-gun troop, a unit he believed would fill a need within the Pennsylvania National Guard if the nation went to war. In much the same way that civic-minded leaders once raised troops to fight in the Civil War, Boal persuaded thirty-three men to join what would become the Boal Troop. This volunteer militia group was formally organized at a meeting at his home in May 1916.

On the eastern part of his estate, Theodore Boal established a training site, which became known as Camp Boal. The National Guard was to supply everything but the horses, but it soon

Theodore Davis Boal as a lieutenant at Mount Gretna, Pennsylvania, circa 1916.

became apparent that Boal was paying most of the expenses himself, providing quarters, rations, uniforms, and fifty-five horses. The volunteers drilled without pay, and their enthusiasm and patriotism caused their ranks to swell. Soon the roster numbered seventy-eight men. A good number were faculty members, students, and employees at Pennsylvania State College (now Pennsylvania State University); others were merchants, machinists, clerks, craftsmen, and laborers from the three nearby counties, as well as a farmer and a doctor.

In a series of inspections throughout the summer, the Pennsylvania adjutant general and U.S. Army regulars praised the troop for its thorough training practices. Boal was voted captain of the troop, with George Thompson and Wilbur Leitzel as his lieutenants. By summer's end, the National Guard accepted the new group as the Machine Gun Troop of the 1st Pennsylvania Cavalry, and the new National Guardsmen marched off to a training camp to the patriotic applause of many local residents. A newspaper reported that some 3,000 townspeople turned out to see off the troops, "with flags flying and the Boalsburg and Pine Grove Mills bands playing patriotic selections."

The troop's first deployment as part of the U.S. Army in October was not to Europe, but to the border with Mexico, where revolutionaries led by Pancho Villa were raiding Texas towns. As an innovation, Boal outfitted several trucks with machine guns, possibly the first mounted machine guns in National Guard history. But the punitive U.S. expedition into Mexico under the command of Gen. John J. Pershing failed to subdue Pancho Villa and his band, and the Pennsylvania troops returned from the Mexican border to Camp Boal the following January.

When the United States was provoked into declaring war on the Central Powers on April 6, 1917, all National Guard units, including the Pennsylvania National Guard, were again federalized as part of the U.S. Army. To better prepare themselves for the type of warfare they knew was being fought in Europe, the guardsmen at Camp Boal excavated a battlefield trench complete with a dugout and protected by an entanglement of barbed wire. Using this protective work, they drilled every two weeks in trench warfare. They even conducted a realistic battle exercise with rockets and imitation shell bursts under the direction of Pierre Boal, who had returned home on leave from the

The Boal Troop on maneuvers in front of Mount Nittany, circa 1916. BOAL MANSION MUSEUM

PREPAREDNESS MOVEMENT

Despite U.S. neutrality in the early years of World War I, aggressive action by Germany together with growing U.S. sympathy for the Allies generated an effort designed to strengthen U.S. military forces, called the Preparedness Movement. Two prime movers in this preparedness campaign were former president Theodore Roosevelt and Gen. Leonard Wood, a former chief of staff of the U.S. Army, who was still on active duty.

Convinced that the United States would fight any future wars with citizen-soldiers as well as professionals, Wood and Secretary of War Henry Stimson tried but failed to persuade Congress to establish a permanent reserve training system. The War Department did, however, sponsor summer military camps to train volunteer reservists. These camps existed to train the officers who would become the nucleus of a future army.

Some individuals took action on their own, such as Theodore Boal, who felt strongly that the country should be militarily prepared and formed his own machine-gun troop. In 1916, General Wood came to Boalsburg to support this effort and review the machine-gun troop as part of a preparedness rally held at the Boal estate. Wood's insistence on strengthening defense preparations brought him, as a uniformed officer, to the brink of insubordination and may have kept him from getting a field assignment in Europe when the United States finally mobilized and sent American troops to fight alongside the Allies.

Although the United States entered the war unprepared for battle when Congress declared war on Germany in 1917, the Preparedness Movement's advocacy of universal military training and conscription in wartime had laid the groundwork for the nation's rearmament and for the Selective Service System, which Congress created to raise an army. As a result, the country entered the war with a Regular Army of about 128,000 men. By war's end, the U.S. armed forces numbered almost 5 million men and women in uniform.

THE MACHINE GUN

The machine gun, a weapon that directs a continuous stream of bullets at a target, was developed into a lethal and important armament during World War I. As much as any other weapon, it set the brutal and unrelenting tone of the war. One soldier could fire hundreds of bullets every minute, mowing down an entire platoon with only a few bursts.

Although different versions of a rapid-firing gun had been devised as early as 1718, most were mechanically operated and so unwieldy that they were not suitable for front-line battlefield action. In 1885, American inventor Hiram Maxim demonstrated the world's first automatic and portable machine gun. This was only possible because of the development of a precisely machined, self-contained brass cartridge. Maxim used the energy of each bullet's recoil force to eject the spent cartridge and insert the next bullet. The machine gun could therefore fire until its entire belt of bullets was used up. It could fire some 500 rounds per minute—the firepower of 100 riflemen.

The gas produced by the explosion of powder in each cartridge created a recoil that served to operate the machine-gun mechanism continuously so that no external power was needed. But because of a rapid buildup of heat while firing, the machine gun had to be cooled, usually by water. This was its main drawback. If not cooled continually, the gun would overheat and become inoperative. Consequently, gunners fired machine guns in short rather than sustained bursts. Later, an air-cooled gun was invented to replace the earlier model with its unwieldy water cooling system.

Before World War I, the British tried the Maxim machine gun but did not order many or put it into wide use. The Germans, however, quickly grasped the potential importance of machine guns on the battlefield. By the time war broke out in August 1914, the Germans possessed some 12,000 Maschinengewehr 08 machine guns, a version of Maxim's invention. By contrast, the British and French had only a few hundred equivalent rapid-fire guns.

From the outset, the German Army demonstrated the value of the machine gun by creating separate machine-gun companies to support infantry battalions. The British did not establish their machine-gun corps until October 1915. Until then, the few machine guns available were attached in sections to individual battalions. Only two were allocated to each infantry battalion in 1914.

When established at fixed strong points to cover potential enemy attack routes, the machine gun proved a fearsome defensive weapon. Enemy infantry assaults upon such positions invariably proved costly. On the first day of the Somme Offensive, the British suffered a record 60,000 casualties in a single day of fighting, the great majority lost to the withering fire of machine guns. Later in the war, the

French Army. Later, the troop underwent eight months of additional training with other units at Camp Hancock in Georgia.

The troopers were sent to Europe in May 1918 as Company A of the 107th Machine Gun Battalion of the 28th Infantry Division. The battalion fought in several battle actions, including those at St. Mihiel and the Argonne Forest. Boal himself never commanded the unit in combat, for he had been reassigned as an aide-de-camp to Maj. Gen. Charles M. Clement and later to Maj. Gen. Charles H. Muir, both commanding generals of the 28th Division. Both generals valued Boal's ability to speak French and serve as an interpreter.

Although he was a staff officer, Boal won the Distinguished Service Cross and the French Croix de Guerre for a battle action on September 27, 1918, in which he risked his life under fire. The War Department's citation reads:

U.S. Army Machine Gun Training in World War I. NATIONAL ARCHIVES

rapid-firing machine gun was adapted for use in armored cars and tanks. For airplanes, a synchronizing device enabled the pilot to fire the gun only at safe intervals so as to miss the propeller blades.

The machine gun is among the most important technologies developed in the last hundred years. As a result of its invention, military strategists had to rethink battlefield tactics that had been used for many years and rely more on aircraft and tanks. It has remained a powerful and effective military weapon ever since. Now rapid-firing submachine guns using the same basic principles can be carried into battle by a single soldier. The latest machine-gun designs incorporate recent advances in ammunition and use computerized targeting.

He voluntarily exposed himself to great danger by repeatedly crossing an elevation swept by extremely heavy fire from rifles and machine guns in order to carry information to some 37-millimeter guns that were enabled to neutralize the machine guns of the enemy which were enfilading the entire front line of the division. His actions were an important factor in the destruction of the hostile machine guns and contributed materially to the success of the attack on the enemy position.

ORIGIN OF THE PENNSYLVANIA MILITARY MUSEUM

By the time the war ended in November 1918, twelve men from machine-gun Company A had been killed in action. Even before the division left France, an officers association was formed, and Boal offered his estate as the site for a reunion of Company A's officers. He had shipped back from France a number of relics, weapons, and souvenirs from the battlefield, which are now in

39

the Boal Mansion. At the first reunion on the Boal estate in 1919, a monument was dedicated to the memory of the twelve fallen troopers. Its inscription reads:

This simple stone cross, found broken in the debris of an obliterated French village through which our troops passed, is erected to the memory of Hayes M. Wilson, Bromley R. Smith, Eugene R. Davis, Michael A. Miller, Donald J. Hile, Arthur Monroe, Ralph I. Dunlap, Claude K. Kahle, William C. Conway, Lewis Crosovalt, James Thorp, and George Simcox. They died in France for liberty.

When Nittany Post 245 of the American Legion was organized in September 1919, Boal was elected its first commander. The officers' club met again on the estate in 1920. The next year, the reunion was broadened to include both officers and men of the entire 28th Division. Shortly thereafter, a separately administered officers' club and permanent barracks and stable for the cavalry troop were constructed. Throughout the 1920s, the camp continued to serve as an active-duty cavalry training ground for the Pennsylvania National Guard. The shrine and club were separately and privately administered. They encouraged the creation of memorials to the 28th Division unit. In 1931, the officers' club and shrine areas, a total of sixty-seven acres, were purchased by the state for the Department of Military Affairs. In 1934, the Society of the 28th Division was formed. It administered the shrine site for the state. Additional monuments were later erected, and a Memory Wall was dedicated after World War II to honor 28th Division officers who were

Dedication of the General Sigerfoos and General Miner Memorials, circa 1924. BOAL FAMILY PAPERS, PENNSYLVANIA STATE UNIVERSITY

Annual Memorial Service. *National Guardsmen of the 28th Infantry (Mechanized) render honors at the division shrine in May 2003.* PENNSYLVANIA MILITARY MUSEUM

killed in World War I. A World War II shrine to commemorate the Keystone Division was added later.

In 1957, administration of the site was transferred to the Pennsylvania Historical and Museum Commission to be developed into a military history museum. The club was torn down in the mid-1960s.

The Pennsylvania Military Museum was constructed and opened to the public in 1969. It featured a replica of a World War I trench and was one of the first dioramic exhibits in the country to include battle sounds. Recently, the museum was totally rebuilt and reopened in 2005. Over the years, tens of thousands of schoolchildren and adults have viewed the museum's exhibits and attended special events on its grounds. In the 1990s, its exhibits were broadened in focus to portray the actions of all branches of the armed forces, as well as the full panorama of conflicts in which Pennsylvanians have fought.

Visiting the Site

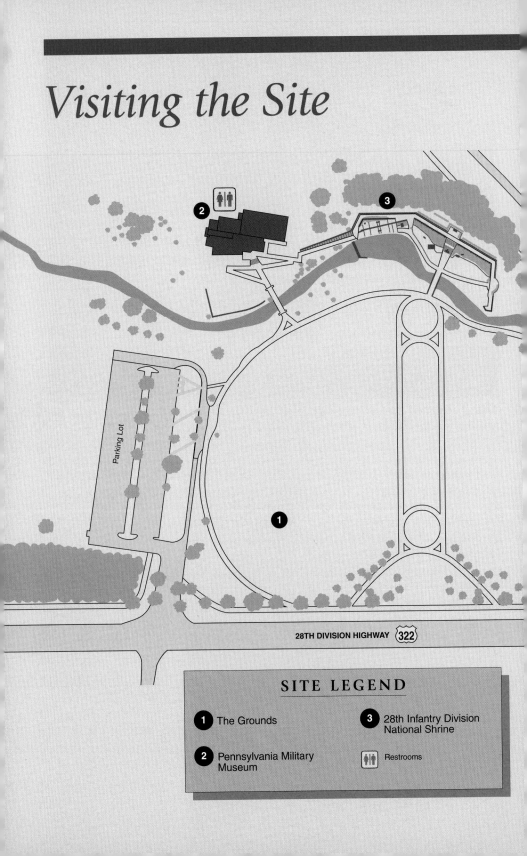

Parking Lot

28TH DIVISION HIGHWAY (322)

SITE LEGEND

1 The Grounds

2 Pennsylvania Military Museum

3 28th Infantry Division National Shrine

👫 Restrooms

1 THE GROUNDS

Visitors stroll the grounds where cavalrymen of the Boal Troop once drilled in preparation for their World War I service in France. A World War II Sherman tank is located in the woods by the front entrance, a memorial suggested by Gen. Norman D. Cota, who led the 28th Infantry Division in World War II. Armored vehicles and artillery pieces dot the landscaped area that stretches in front of the museum. During patriotic observances held occasionally on the museum grounds, reenactment groups bivouac and demonstrate infantry tactics or the loading and firing of artillery.

② PENNSYLVANIA MILITARY MUSEUM

Visitors approach the Pennsylvania Military Museum over a bridge that leads to the main museum building. The colorful front facade, which won an award for its architects, presents an innovative design of military campaign and service ribbons awarded by various branches. In 2004, the museum was expanded, enhancing visitors' learning experience, reconfiguring exhibit space, and providing more artifact preparation and workspace. On entering the building, visitors find an information desk, museum store, and orientation theater. Exhibit galleries examine the tactics and logistics of warfare and feature artillery, armor, infantry weapons, and transportation equipment from the eighteenth to the twenty-first century, including equipment of the U.S. Army, Navy, Marines, Coast Guard, and Air Force.

Future galleries will focus on Pennsylvania soldiers, featuring biographies of those who served during the major conflicts of the last two centuries.

PENNSYLVANIA HISTORICAL
AND MUSEUM COMMISSION

44

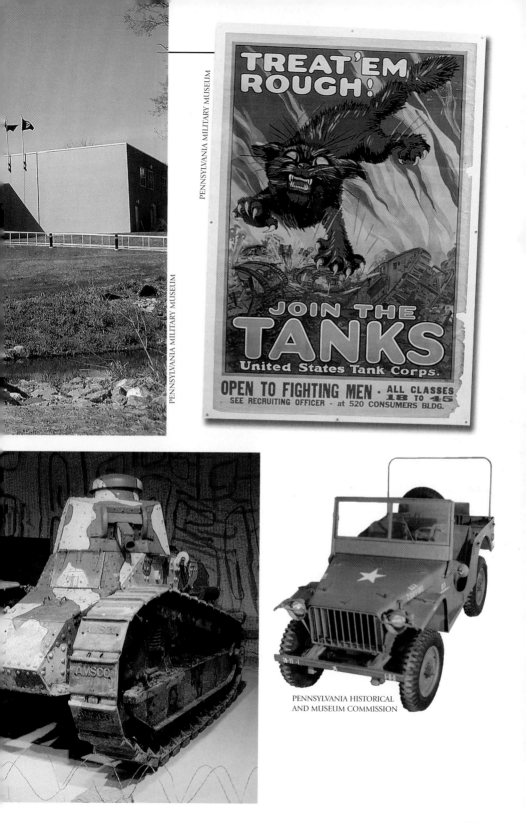

TREAT 'EM ROUGH!

JOIN THE TANKS

United States Tank Corps.

OPEN TO FIGHTING MEN · **ALL CLASSES 18 TO 45**
SEE RECRUITING OFFICER - at 520 CONSUMERS BLDG.

PENNSYLVANIA HISTORICAL
AND MUSEUM COMMISSION

3 28TH INFANTRY DIVISION NATIONAL SHRINE

The expansive shrine area commemorates the citizen-soldiers of the division. A shallow brook winds between the memorials that honor Pennsylvania's military units, dating back to the Revolutionary War. Many of the monuments were placed on the grounds between 1948 and 1956 and include commemoratives to the 109th, 110th, 111th, and 112th Infantry Regiments and the 107th and 108th Field Artillery Regiments. The distinctive 107th Field Artillery Memorial is topped by an artillery shell that is illuminiated at dusk. Visitors are encouraged to observe closely the positioning of these World War I memorials in relation to the creek; the monuments are placed at points that correspond to the units' relative locations in France during the bitter and bloody Argonne Forest Offensive along the Vesle River in August and September 1918.

A double tier of limestone memorial walls stretches in front of a background of trees. The walls are dedicated to Pennsylvanians who died while serving in the two world wars. The World War I Memory Wall holds the names of 114 selected officers of the 28th Division who died in battle; the lower World War II wall, dedicated in 1997, contains the names of all the Keystone Division's enlisted and officer personnel who perished.

A French roadside cross tops a memorial to Brig. Gen. Edward Sigerfoos, who was mortally wounded at Montblainville, the only American general killed in World War I. A German 77-millimeter cannon captured on the battlefield recalls the severe wounding of Gen. Asher Miner in the same conflict. The latest monument to be added to the shrine is the 109th Field Artillery Train Wreck Memorial, from the Korean War era. It honors thirty-three National Guardsmen from northeast Pennsyl-

vania who were killed in the summer of 1950 when their transport train was struck from behind by a passenger train at Coshocton, Ohio, while en route to an Indiana training camp in preparation for the Korean battlefield.

The first monument to be installed at Boalsburg is not included in the shrine area. On August 30, 1919, after the 28th Division had returned from France, veteran officers held a reunion on the grounds of Col. Theodore Boal's estate, where they dedicated an inscribed monument of a cross to the memory of the twelve Boal Troop members killed in action. The present monument stands at the entrance to the Boal Museum, which was the original camp entrance before Route 322 was established.

For more information on hours, tours, programs, and activities at Pennsylvania Military Museum, visit **www.psu.edu/dept/aerospace/museum** or call **814-466-6263**.

Further Reading

Barbeau, Arthur E., and Henri Floretti. *The Unknown Soldiers: Black American Troops in World War I.* Philadelphia: Temple University Press, 1974.

Ferrell, Robert M. *Woodrow Wilson and World War I, 1917–1921.* New York: Harper and Row, 1985.

Gavin, Lettie. *American Women in World War I: They Also Served.* Niwot, Colo.: University Press of Colorado, 1997.

Lansing, Michael Lee. *The African-American Soldier: From Crispus Attucks to Colin Powell.* Secaucus, N.J.: Carol Publishing Group, 1997.

Lockman, Brian, ed. *World War II In Their Own Words: An Oral History of Pennsylvania's Veterans.* Mechanicsburg, Pa.: Stackpole Books, 2005.

Martin, Edward. *The 28th Division: Pennsylvania's Guard in the World War.* 5 vols. Pittsburgh: 28th Division, 1929.

Miller, Arthur P., and Marjorie L. Miller. *Pennsylvania Battlefields and Military Landmarks.* Mechanicsburg, Pa.: Stackpole Books, 2000.

Miller, Randall M., and William Pencak, eds. *Pennsylvania: A History of the Commonwealth.* University Park, Pa.: Pennsylvania State University Press; Harrisburg, Pa.: Pennsylvania Historical and Museum Commission, 2002.

Millet, Allan R. *"Semper Fidelis": The History of the U.S. Marine Corps.* New York: Free Press, 1986.

Newland, Samuel J. *The Pennsylvania Militia: The Early Years, 1669–1792.* Annville, Pa.: Commonwealth of Pennsylvania, Department of Military and Veterans Affairs, 1997.

Sauers, Richard A. *Pennsylvania in the Spanish-American War.* Harrisburg, Pa.: Pennsylvania Capitol Preservation Committee, 1998.

West, J. Martin, ed. *War for Empire in Western Pennsylvania.* Ligonier, Pa.: Fort Ligonier Association, 1993.

Also Available

Anthracite Heritage Museum
and Scranton Iron Furnaces

Brandywine Battlefield Park

Bushy Run Battlefield

Conrad Weiser Homestead

Cornwall Iron Furnace

Daniel Boone Homestead

Drake Well Museum and Park

Eckley Miners' Village

Ephrata Cloister

Erie Maritime Museum and
U.S. Brig Niagara

Fort Pitt Museum

Graeme Park

Hope Lodge and Mather Mill

Joseph Priestley House

Landis Valley Museum

Old Economy Village

Pennsbury Manor

Pennsylvania Lumber Museum

Railroad Museum of Pennsylvania

Somerset Historical Center

The State Museum of Pennsylvania

Washington Crossing Historic Park

All titles are $10, plus shipping,
from Stackpole Books, 800-732-3669, www.stackpolebooks.com, or
The Pennsylvania Historical and Museum Commission, 800-747-7790,
www.phmc.state.pa.us